The East Harlem
Jiu Jitsu Club

PaulJames A. Bekanich &

Julia Fragias

"Impossible is just a big word thrown around by small men who find it easier to live in the world they've been given, than to explore the power they have to change it. Impossible is not a fact. It's an opinion. Impossible is not a declaration. It's a dare. Impossible is potential. Impossible is temporary. Impossible is nothing."
- Muhammad Ali

CHAPTER 1 – The first day...

"Each human being was given two qualities: power and a gift. Power directs us toward our destiny; the gift obliges us to share with others what is best in us."

-Paulo Coelho

The alarm rang.

Seriously?

It was 5:27 am. Anything earlier than 6, I considered the night before, but as I fumbled for the snooze button about ready to knock the thing off its rocker, it hit me.

I chose this?!

Only six months earlier, I was living in the fresh mountain air of Salt Lake City, Utah; a city of serenity located in the northeast corner of the Salt Lake Valley surrounded by the Great Salt Lake to the northwest and embraced by the majestic Wasatch and Oquirrh mountain ranges on the eastern and southwestern borders. I had married a beautiful and intelligent Brazilian woman and was working for the Olympics with a group of mission driven individuals from all over the world. I was training at a small Jiu Jitsu gym with former University of Utah football players. I was competing and winning tournaments. Most days I drove with the top down on my Jeep Wrangler just taking it all in and loving life.

The alarm rang a second time.

5:37 am.

If I hit the snooze again, there would be no way I would make it in time. The commute alone was a circus – 3 subway transfers just to get up to 125th Street in East Harlem followed by a ¾ mile walk, which maybe left enough time to get the desks arranged for the first day of school.

But, I chose this.

* * *

I had convinced myself that I would be the teacher who talks to my kids and not through them. I refused to believe that these students could not or would not do the same work students in the high performing schools around the city and state were expected to do. I was fired up.

When I arrived at the school that morning, I encountered another reality.

Damn, who am I fooling? I don't even know what I'm doing.

I had taught history for two months over the summer at a high school without a lead teacher. She inexplicably left during the middle of the French Revolution and they allowed me to continue teaching despite the lack of support.

I was in utter disbelief. How or what was I supposed to teach these kids? Why should they even care about this content? *Okay class, today we are going to talk about what happens when an elite group of very rich white people ignore the problems of people struggling to make ends meet and have a quality life. Partner up with the person next to you and discuss...*

I started the lesson using the few helpful tools I learned during the early days of teaching. Most of the students bought into what I was saying and I was amazed at how the questions I offered up seemed to engage them as well as they did. It didn't take long; however, for my trance of engagement to wear off. Something started brewing in the back of the class and I had to call it out.

"Hey, everything good back there?" I asked.

A group of boys were completely off task. The most vocal one, who deemed himself the de-facto leader, spoke up for the group. He responded to my question with, "Yeah, son. It's all good."

Yeah, son?

Okay, first, I'm a grown man.

Second, I'm glad you're talking but you will be more successful in here if you are all actually talking about the subject.

I knew how canned and rehearsed it all sounded in my head, but I hoped once I said it out loud it wouldn't come off that way. And so, I did. As I walked away, his response was, "Whatever, bruh."

In that moment, I was hit by two different reactions.

The man in me wanted to yell, "Who does this disrespectful punk ass child think he's talking to?"

The freshly trained teacher in me thought, "Ohhh. I got this!"

I walked back to the boy and took a knee next to his chair.

"Listen, this is unacceptable. I would like you to stay, but if the nonsense keeps up you've got to go. Got it?"

Not a word was heard in my class.

The boy responded, "Yo. What he say?"

Another student spoke up. "Nothing, just do your work. Yo, mista, you a cop?"

"No sir, I am a teacher," I coolly responded as I walked away. I had survived my baptism by fire. I was simultaneously elated that I had their attention and also slightly concerned that maybe I had come off too authoritarian. Either way, I had gotten the boys back on task.

Let's do this!

* * *

"Good morning! Good morning!" I said as I stood by the door of my room to watch my 9th grade Global Studies class enter.

I thought to myself how we were all new to the school. I took solace in that fact and that maybe they were just as scared as I was, although masked by my exuberant greetings. Then again, my 9th graders had just braved the NYC mass transit system and the perils of the crime ridden housing projects to arrive before 8 am. Maybe they weren't that scared.

Somehow between handing out the course syllabus and an introductory discussion on power, one of the students suddenly shouted, "Yo, you fight??"

Shit.

Rule number 1 – don't turn your back on freshmen. While I was circulating the classroom, delivering my inspiring diatribe, a student had slipped behind me and was now, seated at my desk going through my pictures. The one he honed in on was of me with a trophy I won at the Maine State Grapplers Open. I trained 3 months for that fight. I travelled from Utah alone to beat out 5 guys for that trophy. The picture was a testament to how sacrifices do pay off, how anything that is truly worth doing comes with a level of pain and how that pain in turn leads to victory.

How am I supposed to answer this kid?

"Yes, I enjoy the sporting aspects of training and competing." Although it may have sounded corny to my 9th grade audience, it was true. "It's Brazilian Jiu Jitsu. You might have seen some of it if you watch the UFC. It's the ground fighting style a lot of guys use, like wrestling or Judo."

A few excited, somewhat intrigued voices piped up, "Are you gonna teach it? Like, teach it here at school?"

I did not get into education to teach Global Studies. I did not choose education as a career because I was some kind of academic. If anything, I treated high school and college like an athletic and social event. Family and friends called me Peter Pan because I never took life that seriously. There were reasons for that element of my personality that were rooted in some pretty dark childhood events. Education was a viable vehicle to reach kids and help them reach their full potential. I wanted to be that supportive force for them, as others had been for me. I grew up in a single parent household under the conditions of situational poverty. Brown boxed government cheese, dry milk and an endless supply of frozen Pathmark broccoli. But I always knew there was a way out. My mom put herself through college and found meaning in helping others as a social worker. Education transformed her from an immobile shell of depression into a provider for her family of four and the best role model I could hope for.

Their question, "Are you gonna teach it? Like, teach it here at school?" sparked the idea that through this forum these kids could be reached; could be supported. I didn't know how it would come together or what our relationships would look like, but I knew this was a way.

CHAPTER 2 – If you build it, they will come...

It sounded insane - an afterschool martial arts club in East Harlem.

It would be a hard sell to parents, administration and staff that this was not a "fight club." Even more important was to convince the kids that this club was not about fighting.

Logistically, the possibility was bleak. The school itself was housed on one floor and shared its gym with four other schools. Yes, four. It possessed 4 tumbling mats that looked about 35 years old with holes the size of basketballs in them. The administration had limited visibility and no financial support for such a thing. The only positive was the significant level of student interest. Since that first day of school, 15 students from across grade levels had asked about joining. They had even written a petition to the principal to give the green light, but she was probably trying to figure out what Jiu Jitsu was in the first place. Another positive.

And yet, I still believed I could make this untested initiative happen. Like I said, insane.

As interest spread, I ironed out the overall vision and purpose of the club through explaining it to death to my new, unconvinced colleagues. I was going to take the students who had a history of failure and socially maladaptive behaviors and put them in difficult situations that provided them options and opportunities to succeed. Jiu Jitsu would be a teaching tool to provide them the skills they could use in life. The more I talked about it, the more I convinced myself that the most important elements of success for these students – zero-oppositional behavior, academic growth and achievement – were all possible through Jiu Jitsu. And my colleagues soon agreed. The teacher's union, though, wasn't so keen on the idea. Along with not having the money to provide mats, training equipment or a space to train, they also did not have the funds to provide me with a salary. This was a problem, since accepting an un-paid position set some kind of precedent that all teachers would be expected to do the same.

When the union representative came to confront me, I asked her flatly if she felt after school clubs were good for kids. She said yes. That was all I needed to hear. The conversation ended there. This wasn't about the money or the salary. This club **needed** to happen.

* * *

On the subway ride home, I overheard the answer to my logistical obstacles.

A young woman exclaimed to her friend, "I just got my lab equipment today!"

Her friend responded. "Wow that was fast. How long did it take? You requested it like a month ago." I noticed her bag was overflowing with papers marked in black and red ink. They were teachers, too.

"Six weeks. It was so easy...and now, we can do dissections this year!"

I immediately butted into their conversation and asked how she got the money for her equipment. She gave me the name of a donor based website and added that many of her colleagues had gotten the supplies they needed, even sporting equipment, from donors using this site. All I needed to do was write a compelling story of inner city kids needing extracurricular activities to motivate attendance, teach life skills and provide an alternative to street violence. I thanked her and sped on home. I knew there would be many late nights ahead of me, not necessarily ideal for my home life as my wife pointed out. However, this club had the potential of improving the lives of my students both inside and outside the classroom. I hit send on my proposal for $5000 worth of wrestling mats over that weekend and crossed my fingers.

* * *

It was an incredible phenomenon.

Once word got out that the school would have a "fight" team it spread like wildfire. I had random students from every grade coming to me on my breaks asking about it. I saw a mixture of fear, excitement and genuine interest in their faces. Having been a part of some amazing MMA teams in the past, I knew what to look for in potential members. A lot of these teenage boys were more misunderstood than they were a risk to others. They needed focused attention and direction. They needed to agree to and follow the cardinal tenants of Jiu Jitsu. I knew I had to go the extra mile in my selection of students, but also in mentally and physically preparing them to be a team. I honestly had no idea what I was in for.

Things began moving so fast that waiting for the new wrestling mats to come through was not an option. We would have to make do with the raggedy gymnastic mats the school possessed. I pulled them all from the gymnasium and lugged them into my classroom before school started. Permission slips and posters were printed up for students to sign up. My fellow teachers cynically noted how these kids say a lot of things, but they would not show up for try-outs.

Well, at 3:20 pm in mid October I had 40 young men show up.

"Gentlemen, thank you for coming."

I laid out my expectations, so they knew what being a part of this club meant. There were three basic rules that I was serious about upholding and I announced them to this group, in order.

"**Rule number 1** – Under no circumstances will you use anything I teach you here during our time training to fight in life. There should be NO misunderstandings here. It's very straightforward. Do you all understand?"

They responded with a firm and unanimous, "Yes, Sir!" This was a far cry from the "Son" and "Mista" I had been called for the last six weeks. This shift of respect showed me how much they valued the program already.

"**Rule number 2** – When we train, we train as a family. There are no egos in the room. Leave them at the door. You may be surprised by the little guy that taps you, the younger kid that consistently gets the best of you, but like a family, all of that stays in here. We don't hype it up to the rest of the school. We do not embrace the drama that will jeopardize each other or the club. We take care of and support each other's growth. Iron forges iron. The stronger one gets, the stronger we ALL get."

Another firm and unanimous, "Yes, Sir!!"

"**Rule number 3** – When we compete in a tournament, we fight like champions. There are not going to be a lot of kids there that look like you. Most will be white, most will be from the burbs and most will have on fancy gear. It will not matter. We will out train, out work and out think our opponents. We will constantly be working to strengthen our bodies, minds and spirits. When we win, we will win with humility. When we lose, you will lose graciously in front of the crowd, but in private, we will collectively lose it as a team. We do that because we should care about losing and feel safe enough to show it amongst each other.

I let them know we didn't have quality mats yet and they could have cared less. All they wanted to do was start training. I announced that practice would be 5 days a week from 3 to 5 pm.

They were amped.

Let's do this!

That first day was conditioning and drills. Almost none of these kids owned a pair of running shorts. A very few possessed any kind of gym clothing. It didn't seem to matter to them. Picture a parade of 40 young men running the streets of East Harlem in jeans and Timberland boots. That was my team.

Five minutes into the run, there were pleas for water. Another student lamented that his legs hurt. A few seconds later, another one asked if we were done yet.

Are you shitting me?

The toughest kids in school were struggling to run a mile and complaining about it too? This was ridiculous and not what I expected to see from them. I thought about my high school soccer coach and what his reaction would have been had I said, "Coach, I'm tired." He would have told me, "Okay, kid. Go home and sleep. Oh, and pack up your locker when you're done."

I was annoyed, but I realized these kids were untrained. I was going to have to teach them how to endure minor physical trials like, say, this two mile challenge.

"Pain is weakness leaving the body!" I hollered. "Repeatttttttttttttttttttttttt!"

They did. Little by little, one started to encourage the other to push and get through it.

"We got this!" shouted one kid.

After awhile, they started making up their own chants and sure enough, they pushed and finished the two miles.

Back on the mats, I announced we would begin with basic arm locks from a cross body position. Of course, this prompted more than a few "A Yo" and giggles from these guys. Jiu Jitsu, like wrestling, was an up close sport. Add the word "body" in there and this could have been a recipe for disaster. However, getting these East Harlem teenagers over the names of these positions wasn't that difficult once they felt the pain of and the potential of inflicting pain in them.

"Jiu Jitsu is the truth!" A student shouted after a demonstration of 5 arms bars from one initial starting position.

Isn't it...

"This is a mental game, gentlemen. Contingent upon where the arms lands, you will have different options. Dependent on your opponent's movement, you will attempt a different submission. We are not looking for an overhand haymaker knock out. Not that that wouldn't be effective, but what we want is to increase our percentages of a finish. We want to be able to analyze a scenario and develop our own solutions to solving the problem we have in front of us. That is accomplished by using the best technique for the situation and out-thinking our opponents counter."

Ramon, a giant of a child with an inquisitive mind, asked, "How do we know which is best?"

"Excellent question, young warrior scholar," I said.

This was how I regarded them. They needed to be called out. Named.

"Time, practice, persistence, listening and learning from everyone who has something to teach."

Most of them practiced on the floor, since mat space was so limited. No one complained about being tired or thirsty. We had collectively outgrown the episode from the run and all were keyed into training. That was the beginning of the mental journey into Jiu Jitsu for our team.

CHAPTER 3 – Dedication...

Basketball season started in October. It was the one sport at the school that had a strong tradition of participation and a history of excellence. As a result, my initial 40 boys reduced in numbers. Thankfully, the coach of the basketball team, George, a wicked mentor and dean on and off the court, was a **huge** advocate of the Jiu Jitsu program and did not have a problem with his players cross training if basketball were not in session. This is how I got my dedicated twelve. Among them were Steven, Kevin, Scyhine (Za), George, Brice and Ramon. These boys brought something special to the table and left a lasting impression, with me still to this day.

Steven was a 6 foot, 140 pound light skinned Puerto Rican. Some of the students referred to him as "white boy", which he took as neither an insult nor a compliment. His ground game, the way he was able to contort his body and create angles, posed difficult riddles for his opponents to figure out before they were either swept or submitted. He was intense. His parents sometimes struggled with alcoholism and seemed to pop in and out of his life. He had a little brother who he would die for in a heartbeat. He was incredibly loyal. Steven had some trouble making it to school on a regular basis, so I made him my teaching assistant as a way to encourage his regular attendance. Steven hadn't experienced a lot of success at school and didn't play any traditional sports. He really didn't know what it was like to have one successful area in life spill into others, what I called success breeding success. At least, not until he joined our team. Tough guys would see this skinny kid and expect that they could ball him up. Steven would extend a hand and a smile, then proceed to ball **them** up. This kid could roll! Not only did he give our team credibility, but it made Steven's self esteem sky rocket.

George, described by some of his peers as "roly-poly", was a 5 foot 8", 200 pound Jamaican. He was an excellent academic student and this brilliance translated well to his ground game. In contrast, laziness, one of his biggest challenges, also manifested itself in his Jiu Jitsu. If there was an easy way to do something that didn't require more than 80% of his energy and commitment, he would be fine with that 80%. He also sometimes stopped trying to think when stuck in a difficult position. It was as if he gave up hope too soon, never realizing how good he actually was. And yet, George was always enthusiastic to train and was never intimidated by the number of people on the mats. His unintimidating physique and command of solid positions made him the perfect introduction to club newcomers and a great tutor.

Having Steven and George on our team was like a double personification of the core mission of Jiu Jitsu. Royce Gracie, the ambassador of Brazilian Jiu Jitsu, and his family brought the art of Brazilian Jiu Jitsu into the martial arts world and eventually main stream America. The Gracies wanted to show the world that physical size and strength did not determine the winner. They created a style of grappling that focused on leverage and manipulation, which made even a small, less athletic person a level contender against a more imposing figure. It was through choosing Royce, who had such a build, to get the message across that allowed the "gentle art" of Jiu Jitsu to be recognized as an extremely effective tool in both self defense and sport fighting. My boys represented that same look of beat-a-bility. They were humble, unassuming and never looking for a fight. But, to use Royce Gracie's own words, if you put them on the mat and the devil was on the other side, they would come out there to win. I wanted all my kids to gain that understanding and value.

Brice was my man child at over 6 feet and 250 pounds. He was a gentle giant with a heart of gold; that is, until you pissed him off. When bathed in a sea of calm, he was a shoulder to lean on and a great training partner. When pissed, he would smash you through tears of rage. We all discovered this on more than one occasion. His ragefulness was like a trance I had to walk and talk him out of to bring him back to reality and back to the mats. Typically, I would be the one to roll with him, since most of the guys did not want to be the recipient of his wrath. Funny thing was he just couldn't bring himself to hurt anyone or inflict the kind of damage he was known for **unless** he was genuinely angry. Finding a balance between these extremes posed an obstacle for him.

Scyhine or Za, as he was called by most, was a physical specimen at 5 foot 11" with single digit body fat. He was fast and flexible. His interest was driven by being social more than competing. Although he was disciplined, he sometimes let his emotions get the best of him. Za played things close to the chest, never asked for help and remained an enigma in many ways to me, despite the bonds and experiences we shared.

Kevin was and continues to be one of the most focused individuals I have ever known. He was completely devoted to perfection. Disciplined in every aspect of his life, this was also reflected in his ground game. Kevin could have dominated in whatever sport he chose. Selfishly, I was glad he had chosen Jiu Jitsu over basketball or we would have lost a great talent. Unlike many of his fellow team members, Kevin lived with both his parents and had a strong supportive bond to his family. He was completely devoted to them and strove to make them proud of whatever endeavor he was involved with. He never looked for a fight, but if one presented itself, he wouldn't back down. City life, especially his neck of the woods, gave him strength. He used his experiences to build fortitude and focus.

Ramon was, like Brice, another giant at 6 foot 4" and 250 pounds. If he were in a suburban school, they probably would have pegged him for an offensive lineman. He was so much more than that. He was an old soul; wise beyond his years with a sharp mind and rapier wit. He consistently had the team laughing at one of his random thoughts, which would interrupt conversation at the most unlikely of moments. In addition to his physical prowess, this kid had a talent for visual art and even designed our team shirt. Ramon was our Renaissance man.

* * *

The program was in its seventh week and everything had been progressing surprisingly well. I was chatting with some of my colleagues about the looming Halloween holiday and the potential of gang initiations, fights and general misconduct. I learned that a few years prior there had been a gang fight right in front of the school. I found it a shame that the good students were prevented from wearing costumes or having any kind of party due to the threat of a few. I expressed this to them, only to be met with condescending glares and a few sympathetic nods at my optimism.

The intercom disrupted our conversation.

"PJ, please come down to the main office."

Oh, crap. What did I do now?

Since starting this job, I had been chastised by the Assistant Principal for using too much paper to print out resources to supplement the outdated 35 year old textbook I was given, challenged by the union for my role as coach/teacher of my Jiu Jitsu team when I wasn't receiving a salary for it and reprimanded by a regional superintendent for commenting on the lack of protocols for removing a student from class. I could only imagine who else I had pissed off doing what I believed was best for these kids.

I made my way to the main office.

"You have a delivery downstairs," the secretary stated flatly without looking up at me.

Relief.

Glistening their bright orange veneer of newness in the afternoon sun, were my 5 large wrestling mats. The donor site had finally come through. I inhaled their new mat scent like that of fresh laundry. The smell of anything new in this school was an anomaly, so this really caused a commotion. I shouted to two of my Jiu Jitsu students to give me a hand.

"New mats! Let's go, gentleman," I told them with a huge grin.

With the help of two more of my students, we carried them up the three flights of stairs. The students we passed were curious to know what they were. As my boys proudly filled them in, they received supportive congrats on the new equipment. That afternoon practice saw some of the most epic battles ever waged. These kids had previously trained on those decrepit torn mats, on Astroturf in a recreational center and even on the grass in Central Park. Now, they took advantage of this foreign soft landing surface to attempt rolling knee bars and flying triangles. Take downs were plentiful. Kids smiled through the sweat, submission attempts and taps. As class wound down, George asked for a couple of minutes to address the squad. I let him, without asking why. I was curious to hear what he had to say.

"Guys, there is a tournament after Thanksgiving and I want to go. Anybody interested?" He asked eagerly.

As I watched their eyes widen and their energy kick up about fifty notches, my first reaction was *Oh shit.* Were they good enough for a tournament? Would they be embarrassed in front of these other, more elite schools? Would they be able to handle it if they lost? Then, I questioned if I was even a good enough coach to place them in a tournament.

"What do you think, coach?" asked Kevin.

Their desire to compete switched off my anxiety fueled thinking.

"Gentlemen, I think we have trained our asses off for the last two months. I cannot believe all the growth I've seen, not just as fighters but as people. I think we are a strong team. I'd be honored to coach you guys."

It was decided. The only question now was how to get the money we needed for entry fees and expenses. George came up with the idea of a bake sale and pizza selling party, both of which were approved. I often lamented the lack of parental involvement at our high school level and assumed this would be the case for both fundraisers. A few dozen phone calls and strategically sent emails later, and many parents turned out to support our efforts.

We ended up raising enough money for **three** entry fees. After writing to the director of the tournament about our situation, we were also granted two additional spots for free. The universe always delivers for those who attempt to walk the right path. Now, it just needed to deliver a way for all of us to get there.

* * *

There are things we do in life just for love – for the love of the game, the team and camaraderie, the vision of bringing some good into the world. These choices sometimes defy logic. We give up time with our loved ones, financial gain by giving away things that are a cost to ourselves and at times our physical safety and health by taking risks that others might think unnecessary. The rewards for doing things solely out of love are priceless.

Andrew was the school computer guy. Still in his early twenties, he was in many ways a big kid himself. He grew up in the worst of circumstances without any formal education and yet, he acted like a mentor, big brother and student advocate on so many levels. He was legitimately vested in the lives of the students. He even trained with our club on more than one occasion. This is why when he heard we needed a ride to the tournament, he quickly offered himself up.

The weeks leading up to the tournament were intense. We practiced for 2 hours after school every day and Saturdays for conditioning. No one missed a day of school. No one missed a practice. We chose the students who would represent us – Kevin, Za, Steven, George and a young man named Miguel. The once apathetic student body now had a team outside of basketball to cheer for. These were **our** warriors. My guys had become strong and controlled. They had developed the skills to harness that urban angst and turn it into focused, ferocious determination. They were confident young men on a mission.

We ended our last practice that Friday before Sunday's tournament with our team anthem by Jay Z and Eminem. Andrew, a voracious collector of underground hip-hop singles, had made an iPod mix he called "The Fight" and premiered it on our drive up later that night. It was played on continuous loop. Imagine a clown sized Toyota packed 5 deep in the back with oversized tough guys from the South Bronx and East Harlem driven by a brolic young Italian and shaggy haired white Social Studies' teacher on the passenger side. This motley crew eagerly rolled into Milford, Connecticut on Saturday afternoon completely unprepared for what surrounded them. My kids fell silent, which was especially rare, when they saw the golden staircases, flat screen TV's and indoor pool of our hotel.

"Yo, this is really cool," said George in the elevator ride up to our rooms.

"Yeah, this sweet bro. Thanks, Coach!" added Kevin.

"There's no gum stuck onto the elevator," remarked Steven.

Yup.

It was impossible to get these boys to sleep that night. Even the quasi-glutinous Italian carb load of a dinner they ate, the swims in the indoor pool and hot tub soaks did nothing to mellow them out. Even worse, they had a PlayStation in their room, so their precious rest time was replaced by an all out slaughter on Halo to an unholy hour of the morning. Their excitement clearly made my desire for sleep a distant wish.

Andrew and I decided to order a pizza to soothe our insomnia. We got to talking and after I thanked him for his invaluable role in getting us all to the tournament, he turned to me and said, "It's really cool what you've done with these kids. When you got up here, everybody thought you were crazy. **I** thought you were crazy, but seriously bro. These kids were missing something that they didn't know was missing. You've given them something to come to school for and made them feel a part of something."

"All I did was set up a team. They are setting their own goals," I responded.

My only hope, in that moment, was for our asses not to be handed to us the next day.

* * *

"Good morning, sunshine. You guys up???!!!" I hollered as I entered their room.

Amazingly, Steven announced that everyone had already gone for a run. No sleep; no worries. Ah, the blessings of youth.

They assembled themselves promptly in the lobby at 7:30 am for equipment check. I couldn't help but think about the disparity these kids were about to behold. Many of their competitors were from the wealthier suburbs of New England. They trained at Gracie schools and other well established academies with full time coaches. Their parents uniformed them in Tap-Out clothing without any concern about cost. They had 50 dollar shorts and 60 dollar rash guards from Brazil to train in and all new gear for tournaments, while my kids rolled out mats in an East Harlem classroom with their blue belt level instructor. My kids came in wearing Triple X t-shirts, wife beaters and sweatpants. I had to tell them not to wear jeans during training and especially not to wear them at the tournament, even though jeans may have been their only wardrobe option. My medal chasers were definitely not a part of the Jiu Jitsu consumer culture.

We drove in silence to the tournament. Andrew played our team anthem to get them psyched. By the time the song was over, we were there. I knew I had to give them a pregame speech. The song lyric about running up clubs, poppin' people's heads off probably wasn't a good enough fire starter.

"Gentleman. Warriors. I cannot tell you how proud I am of all of you in this moment. I've seen so much effort given, so much talent developed. You have walked through the pain. You have overcome fear. Just to be here with you right now is an honor! Let's go in there with our heads held up knowing we did everything in our power. Let's represent ourselves and our community well."

"And let's kick some New England ass!!!!!" shouted Kevin.

"YEAHHHHHHHHHHHH!!!!" we all screamed.

As we entered the varsity gym, its massiveness was overwhelming. It dwarfed our single floor school's excuse for a gym by about 1000.

"Yo, where are all the black people?" Za asked George.

We were in a sea of Caucasian.

This was one more challenge to overcome. Even though we had discussed it before, it was a completely jolting experience in actuality to be surrounded by a group of people who look nothing like you in such large numbers. I took them to get weighed in and after figuring out their division placements, it was time to roll. Miguel was up first. He was paired with a smaller kid. They clinched, stumbled to the floor, and Miguel landed on top. Four points for that mount. Not much else happened during the match, but a win was a win.

Za drew a larger kid that looked intimidating. He hit a double leg, transitioned from cross body to mount and executed a technically proficient straight arm bar. Now, we were two for two. I was feeling way more confident about my team and my coaching.

Steven won his first two matches via mata leão from rear mount and triangle from guard. I could hear Andrew squeal from across the gym. Then, an elated Za and Andrew started to recount their wins with the rest of our team as well as kids from other gyms who offered up congratulations. My boys **belonged** here!

Miguel's second match was against a man-child who hit a double leg and finished Miguel in about 15 seconds with a kimura from cross body top. He was out of medal contention; however he did log a win. Miguel was disappointed, but understood he was outmatched. I was proud of how he handled it.

What happened next still haunts me to this day.

Za, who felt strong and confident after his first win, locked up with his second opponent. He proceeded to pick him up, bend his knees and jump like a damn World Wrestling superstar into the air, driving his opponent into the ground.

Thud.

Whistle.

"Disqualified!!!"

"Noooooooooooo," I screamed on the inside. Everything became like a corny slow motion film sequence. I felt helpless as I sprinted toward the mat anticipating what would happen next.

Za completely lost his shit.

"What the fuck man! No, I didn't jump. I took him down. This is BULLSHIT!!"

The hand I attempted to put on his shoulder was aggressively shoved off. As Za continued to have his public meltdown, I called Andrew over to take him to the car. After some argument, he finally went. Then, I was chastised by the tournament director for what happened. Somehow I had to regain my focus on the remaining guys.

I could completely relate to the meltdown Za had. It was at my second tournament, when I was coming off a first place finish, ranking second in the absolute in Maine. My team wasn't present for that win and in retrospect; I probably traveled across the country alone just so that if I lost no one I knew would witness it. This tournament would be the first time I had the support, but also the pressure of the people I bled and sweat with watching me roll. We traveled to Vegas together as a team to compete as a team. My first match so happened to be against an MMA fighter and division one wrestler from our rival school in Salt Lake. Everyone was hyped. We tapped fists and the match was on. He shot in for a double leg. I turned my hips mid flight and took his back. Once we hit the mat, my arms were already in position to sink in the rear naked choke, mata leão and it was over. I have no idea why I kind of kicked him off of me, but I did. I immediately apologized, as both teams ran in to support their fighters. I had to recover from that high immediately and compose myself for the next round. I went in full of confidence. I had my opponent in my guard, raised my hips and attacked the knee.

Pop.pop.

In my arrogance, I left an opening and had my knee and ankle ripped. It wasn't the physical pain that pushed me into a lunacy driven chair throwing rage. It was that I let my friends down. Publicly, I alone was to blame. What Za did was unacceptable, but it would have been absurdly hypocritical to say it wasn't completely understandable.

Then a strange thing happened in Za's division. Miguel was given a chance to continue in Za's spot due to some logistical error. He ended up with a silver medal. Za, despite the disqualification, earned a bronze. The medal went to Miguel's head and this compounded Za's mental state. For years after the match, Miguel acted like some kind of Jiu Jitsu god claiming his medal meant he was better than Za.

Steven won a silver medal after going to war with a far superior grappler. I watched as he shook hands with his opponent and acknowledged the guy's skills. It was a great show of sportsmanship. George also won a match on points and placed third; however, he was up against much bigger guys and realized that it might be smart for him to cut weight properly for next time. Kevin was last and his division was stacked with high school wrestlers and the number 2 ranked kid in the nation, Tom Fox. Kevin had told me he wanted a challenge. He was definitely going to get it with these guys; their size, skills and experience were no joke!

"If I'm going to win, I want to win big!" Kevin exclaimed. "I want to know how good I am and how much work it's gonna take to be the best."

How could you not respect a kid willing to take risks in public and push himself to reach his potential?

During Kevin's first match, he went out into a boxing stance. His opponent took a low wrestler's position and shot in. Kevin sprawled. His opponent put his hand on Kevin's forehead. This movement is not uncommon in wrestling and used to gauge distance; however in East Harlem, this was known as a "mush" – a blatant sign of disrespect.

Shit, here we go again.

I prepared myself for another meltdown of Za proportions. Kevin appeared to keep it together, although he shouted that he was being mushed. I yelled for him to keep to his game. Kevin shot in, mounted and finished with an arm triangle. He begrudgingly shook hands with the other kid.

After questioning me about the mushing and having explained that it was a wrestling move, Kevin excitedly asked, "So, I can do that?"

"Yes, just don't slap him. Gauge distance, got it?"

During the second match, Kevin went to town with the new distance gauging move. It seemed like an eternity of two kids pushing each other's foreheads. Then, Kevin was taken down by the other bigger kid. Kevin pulled guard and scissor swept his opponent, managed an electric chair guard pass to open the legs and cart wheeled into cross body top. Two seconds later, he applied the Americana for the win.

Beautiful.

He had one more match.

"Tom Fox??" he asked excitedly.

"Tom Fox," I replied much less so.

Tom Fox, the aforementioned number 2 in the nation, was a kid from northern Virginia. He was a good kid from a wealthy family, who drove him to tournaments around the country. He won almost every match and had the confidence of a champion. For the first time, I saw Kevin slightly rattled.

"Okay, it's one on one in there, little brother. Go get your gold!"

It was over quickly. Fox with a hip toss. Fox with a mount. Fox having taken mount, left Kevin in a position where he mistakenly extended an arm to push Fox off. Straight arm bar.

Kevin accepted his medal graciously and congratulated Tom and his coach.

"I can be better than that guy. I'm not now. The guy is amazing, but I can beat him." Kevin later told me.

With the exception of Za, everyone felt like a champion. We placed 8th overall in the team competition. A top ten finish after a few Gracie schools, a Lloyd Irvin school and a Link Academy is not a bad first tournament. We were given a champions welcome when we got back to school on Monday morning. Everyone wanted to see the medals and look at the pictures. The team rarely experienced such success or positive attention and they ate it up. Everyone that is, except for Za. While the guys told their stories and smiled from ear to ear, Za was silent. He still couldn't admit to himself that he had lost it. He wouldn't admit he had slammed his opponent even when all his teammates pointed out that he had. He stopped coming to practice after that. Years later, he wrote me a poignant email recalling how deep his struggle with anger had been at that time. The months he had spent in our club were not lost on him, though. In his own words, "What you've given me has always been my reality in the present." He learned to trust himself and to channel his anger into motivation for success. The rest of the team was inspired to train even harder and with a new level of focus. Their success in the tournament yielded another bonus – 100% attendance in school and a 100% pass rate in their grades.

CHAPTER 4 – Know Thyself In Order To Serve

December.

This time of year was especially destabilizing for many of the students in my school. Feelings of abandonment and loneliness permeated the collective consciousness mixed with the yearnings of a Christmas free of chaos and disruption from some. I could relate.

In my early childhood, Christmas was a time of joy, of hiding out under the couch with my little brother trying to catch Santa delivering gifts only to magically wake up in our beds the next morning not knowing how we got there. Of Pappa rolling the old time camera to catch me and my brothers and cousins in our matching footed pyjamas coming out of the bathroom to open our gifts in front of parents, aunts, uncles, cousins, grandparents and grand aunts and uncles. The tree decorated in ornaments we had all made was the center of this family hive of life. We were all connected and covered in a physical and emotional blanket of warmth, security and love.

That blanket was violently ripped off when I was 11. My dad left the family unit. My little brother, sister and I woke up to the shrieks and cries of my mother and a slamming door of her leaving the house. My dad came into our room, saying very little, and drove us to our grandparent's house where we all learned that our world was being torn apart. Although he loved my mom, he wasn't "in love" and he was leaving the house. This trauma was followed up a few months later with an ultimatum posited by my mother. In retrospect, I do not know why or how we kids found out about this but there was another woman. He would either choose his family or the "she devil" (as she became to us) on Christmas Eve. If he came back home, he would be committing to the family. If he didn't show up, he would never be allowed to cross the threshold of our home again. Ever.

I remember the tree lit, my mom in a rocking chair. Waiting...Rocking...Waiting. Hours of this, with every second seeming like a paleolithic eon. I was literally growing up and dying with each passing moment, watching the person responsible for my safety wither in a rocking chair by a fireplace of slowly extinguishing flames and the man of the house vanish like a ghost along with any semblance of security I would ever feel until adulthood.

For the rest of my young life, I felt as if I was walking a tightrope. Any misstep, any fuck up or bad decision meant a horrifying fall into a space of near death, with each impact difficult to recover from. During the next 6 years, it was my extended family that kept any sense of normalcy and sanity for me. The sweet wholesome joy and magic of innocence died that Christmas, but the love that my grandparents et all continued to give never relinquished. My dad and his family virtually disappeared, but my mother's clan stepped up and made things at least manageable for us. This feeling of belonging probably saved me from being a total deviant.

* * *

The days approaching Christmas 2003 were a really good time for my boys. We had just come off the tournament win and our basketball team was making a surprise run deep into the play offs. Since our club was on hiatus until the New Year to recoup, I had the time to join the rest of the community after school to cheer the team to victory.

"Excuse me, sir. Are you enjoying the game today?" asked an 11th grader by the name of Chris. He wasn't one of my students, but I had seen him around school.

"Yeah, thanks," I replied.

"Excellent," he said. "Enjoy." As he walked away from me, he turned to his friend and said something that shocked me.

Motherfuckin' white boy.

I was one of the few white teachers working at the school. I was proud of the fact that I could connect to my students in meaningful ways despite this difference. I was often asked if I were Brazilian, Cuban or anything other than white. I looked at this perception of me as a form of acceptance. However, it also kicked up a feeling of shame for my whiteness. I found myself apologizing from time to time for my race; something I had no control over. This insecurity prevented me from being my authentic self. This was something I had to learn to work hard through in order be present for my kids. I couldn't believe the blatant disrespect this student, Chris, had just shown me. An unexpected rage boiled up inside me. No one up until that point had pointed out the obvious, and stated it with such disgust and venom. *Motherfucker* was bad enough, but it was *white boy* that cut. His comment brought up the harsh reality of how some of these kids **actually** perceived me. It made me feel like an uninvited guest; an invader. Maybe it was entitlement. I had always been accepted. Mormons brought me in. Brazilians initially joked about me being a gringo, but ended up saying my heart was *Brasileiro*. This devastated my confidence. It made me question why I was there and if I could really have a positive influence.

As my land of color blind ignorant bliss continued to implode, I sought out the advice of someone I respected and trusted. Garrett was both a Harvard educated teacher and also a good friend. He told me connections and cultural sensitivity made the difference between teachers and students; not race. I wasn't buying it. I asked him point blank, "If I were the same race as my students, would I be more effective."

"PJ, if there were a Black or Latino you, then I would say yes. There's not. There is just **you**."

* * *

"It is up to us to take responsibility, not because we are guilty but because we are here." -Peter Wise

After some time spent with family in Brazil, I had the ability to reflect on my effectiveness. I vowed to continue working with and mentoring the young men of the East Harlem Jiu Jitsu club. I would not allow what had occurred to devour my spirit. I would not let those cutting words consume me with unwinding emotion. I had to, instead, remain focused on my mission and be patient for the wins, no matter how small or subtle, because they always seemed to come at the right times. As a teacher, you are confronted with all of the challenges faced by society wrapped up in a volatile hormonally driven subculture often misunderstood by the nation as a whole – teenagers. I would not stand down.

It was the morning of the first day back in school from break. With warm cinnamon and sugar oatmeal from the Dominican place in hand, I watched yet another disruption to student life unfolding before me.

"Why is the principal being escorted out of the building?" I asked my colleague.

Urban schools fail for a myriad of reasons. In this case, there were allegations and rumors, but none of us ever heard an official explanation for what happened, nor did we get any protocol for how the school community would function without a leader. The principal was simply gone. Keep calm and carry on.

Teaching and training resumed and within a few weeks, we were all back on a regular schedule. It was then that a group of older white women in suits marched into school. The regional superintendents had arrived to present to us the new principal, a well heeled black woman named Ms. Hardaway.

I soon learned Ms. Hardaway was a true professional. She made genuine attempts to connect with staff and students. She made herself visible in the halls, but not as much in the classrooms. Her focus seemed to be more on restoring and ensuring discipline was the priority. This was understandable. She had inherited a school is chaos, with behavior and academics at an abysmal level; not to mention the removal of its principal for unknown reasons. Although my classroom was never the scene of violence, major disruption or even a Jiu Jitsu club scrap, I knew this was not the school wide norm. Through conversations with students, she learned of our club and the pride it generated throughout the school community. On a Friday afternoon, deep in grading essays, I heard a knock at my door. Without looking up, I waved the person in.

"So, you are teaching students how to fight," Ms. Hardaway said flatly.

Of course, she had every reason to question if our fight club was actually a "fight" club, but I had prepared what I felt was a pretty solid argument.

"That's not how we look at it." I responded. "It is self-defense. A game of physical chess that teaches students not to use force, but strategically counter movements by using their opponents' force in their favor."

Ms. Hardaway's expression did not change.

"It's no more dangerous than wrestling, which a lot of schools support. We train like a team and support each other like a family. Our practice involves social skill development, in addition to physical training. Did you know that there has not been one single fight involving any of my team members? And if there ever were, the consequence would be dismissal from the club. In fact, my students are often trying to diffuse conflict when they come across it."

She did not appear to be impressed at all by my arguments. She wanted to discuss this matter further in her office. It was then that I got scared. Was this it? I had to fight for the team's survival, but what if the only reason I was even able to have such a club was solely because no one was actually running anything in that school. Hardaway was serious. She said very little and her body language even less. She would just let you hang yourself with your own words. I had to speak a language that would resonate with her; the language of objective, fact driven evidence and not my subjective musings. I went to her office and hoped my words would be effective.

I spent the next twenty minutes outlining how Jiu Jitsu increased mental and moral power. This sport taught students how to think; how to move the body and mind as one. There were countless possibilities in one movement and hundreds of counters to a counter. In teaching them how to get out of a disadvantageous position through strategy instead of just giving up, they were learning resiliency. If they could get out of that, then they could tackle other areas in life with the same mindset. The mat was a place of equality and truth. Everyone teaches each other. The smaller student had something to teach the larger one and vice versa. My students pledged to leave their egos at the door. They not only treated each other with respect and humility, but also others. Recently, I had learned from the office manager that four of my boys had come to her aid to carry boxes she was struggling with up the stairs. They did so and told her to have a nice day. She was impressed by their thoughtfulness and conduct and attributed it to their participation in the club. I stressed the consequences laid out for these boys not following the rules or for partying and partaking in unhealthy activities. They all knew the rules, respected them and most importantly, stopped each other from breaking them. The accountability was tremendous. I made my last plea for the club's survival.

"Ms. Hardaway. Please do not make me stop coaching this team. It means too much to them and the school." I thanked her for her time and walked out of the office hoping that her poker face had absorbed all of what I had said.

A few days later, she agreed to support the club. She appointed me a Dean and found a way to pay me for coaching. She wanted everything to be done by the book. Our team was a good face for a school that didn't have many and she made that face official.

* * *

With the Jiu Jitsu Club on solid footing and a winning record, interest peaked again from the basketball players attracting a student named Michael. He was a senior and the kind of kid the girls loved and guys wanted to emulate. He was a good student, a great basketball player on scholarship to a Division 2 school and a really great kid overall. At 6 foot 5" and 220 pounds he would have been a force to be reckoned with on the mats. He rolled occasionally, but mostly came through to discuss UFC, grappling and life in general. The counter to Michael was a friend of his named Carlos. He dealt drugs to junior high kids, was constantly thrown out of classes and generally infamous for his obnoxious attitude. I never had any dealings with him until Michael came into our club.

"Yoooooooo! A yo!" Carlos screamed from outside my overcrowded class of 35. Miraculously, not one head looked up. They were locked into their exams and I moved closer to the door to eliminate the distraction.

"Hey, bro. Can I help you?" I asked. "We're taking a test. Who are you looking for?"

"You that teacher teaching Michael that faggity ass fighting shit?" he asked.

"Ummm, yeah," I replied not put off at all by his attitude. "Why? Did you want to train? We're here 3:00 every day."

"Nahhh, bitch. I don't fight like that." He signaled to his pocket as if to indicate he was carrying or to let me know he would shoot me.

"Hey man. Door is always open," I replied trying to be both teacher and adult, but I couldn't hide my own hostility at this threat. Carlos said something under his breath and walked off.

"Mr. B. Want me to handle that?" My student JG piped up. This kid led a group of Latin Kings and just happened to be one of my favorite students. He had once been shot on a Saturday, but came into school Monday to hand in his paper. When I asked him if the shot was meant for him, he answered maybe him or the guy next to him all nonchalantly. His offer was tempting. I had recently learned I would be a father.

Jiu Jitsu loses to bullets every time.

I couldn't.

I told him to let it go and left school uncharacteristically early that day.

When my wife asked me how my day was, I had to tell her. She was obviously upset and pointed to her belly.

"I know you love these kids, but they are **not** your family. I need you. **WE** need you!"

I agreed with her. I told her I didn't think he was serious and that he was angry at his friend Michael. I just happened to be in the way. Michael and Carlos had a history, which I attempted to explain to her.

"What is the school doing about this?" She interrupted. "You told the director, right?"

I lied to my wife and told her no. Truth was, I had asked Ms. Hardaway to do something. I was worried and wasn't completely convinced Carlos wouldn't try something. This was a fear I wasn't going to express to my already concerned, pregnant wife. In the days that followed, it became clear that Carlos was there to stay. The principal was not going to expel him, nor suspend him for his threat. She had talked to him, as did another teacher, Clover, who had known Carlos since he was a freshman. I had come into the school when Carlos was a senior. Clover, who mentored me in many ways in the beginning, assured me he was more mischievous than dangerous. For the next few weeks, I was on high alert. Carlos mad dogged me every time we passed each other in the hallways and never responded to my attempts to say *what's up*.

When my new car's tires were slashed and the rearview mirrors smashed, Carlos's cousin gave him up as the culprit. Administration did nothing.

"He doesn't fight like that," Clover had said.

"This kid slashed my tires!!!???" I told her. "Are you kidding me? Clover, I have a family. I want this kid gone!"

It's bizarre how quickly something as scary as Carlos's desire to cause me harm could become the norm. I knew nothing could be done about it, so it became a part of my daily consciousness. Then, he was gone. I learned from his cousin he was confronted by someone or a group, depending on who was telling the story, and that he got his arm and nose broken. When Carlos came back to school, he mumbled an apology to me and that was it. I was angry at the lack of boundaries and repercussions for threatening a teacher. I was also deeply upset that this kid, who came from a broken home and had so much adversity in his life, wasn't someone I could help. Shortly after graduating high school, Carlos went to jail. Once again, I was split in my thinking. Part of me thought *good, little fucker got what he deserved* and the other struggled with the fact that I could have done more if I wasn't paralyzed with fear for myself and my family's safety. It was such an unfair situation for both of us, but Carlos paid the ultimate price. To say that January was rough would be a gross understatement. I deeply considered finishing out the year and never returning. Then Steven, the student I had been working with on his midwinter exams, came to me with his passing scores in English and Math.

"Mr. B. Thanks!" he exclaimed.

His *thank you* made the difference for me. I chose to continue.

* * *

"Coach, can we talk?"

Za had been a virtual ghost since his meltdown in November. He was missed by the team and I had asked Kevin if he would be willing to sit down and talk to me. Up until that point, Za had not taken me up on that offer.

"Can I come back?" he asked.

I knew he had needed the time to come to terms with what happened and come up with his own meaning from it. I hoped an authentic change had occurred.

"Yes, but under a few conditions. You made us look bad, bro. I want you back, but I'm not the only one who will be making that decision. If the team approves and you agree to stay focused and listen to me on the mat, you're back in."

We voted the next day and unanimously approved his return. The team agreed Za needed focus and offered to help him. They also offered to get him caught up on all the missed techniques. My pride at how tightly knit this team had become continued to swell.

My boys!

I had organized an open mat day, where students and parents had signed waivers at the beginning of the year to come train with us. I delegated Kevin to lead everyone that had shown up through drills. It was shocking to see how much more flexible and cardio driven our Jiu Jitsu boys were compared to the basketball players.

"Yo, look at George!" said Flood, a well conditioned athlete who was struggling with pushups. George was just cranking them out.

"Okay, gentlemen. Grab a partner and line up." I ensured all visitors that they would be matched with someone who already knew what they were doing for the first round.

As a result, the guys who had experience on the mats dominated the athletes that didn't. A mixture of expressions ranging from confidence to disbelief covered the room; however everyone was smiling. I'm sure many of the visitors were probably happy to tap early and often to keep their arms from being snapped off by my guys.

Next round also saw pairings of experience versus non-experience, except for one. The two boys were friends, so I thought nothing of it. The rolling began and then I heard a kid yell, "Damn bro. I'm sorry. That was my bad!"

I turned and started to ask what happened before I saw the tremendous gash over a kid named Manny's forehead. Manny was my student; a funny kid who spent most of his time off task or not in school. I was glad that he had come to practice that day to get him excited about something school related. This was not good.

"I've got to get you to a clinic, bro!" I said.

He turned to me and said, "Mr. B. I fell outside. I'm not here, so you can't take me anywhere."

I was taken aback. I tried to tell him not to worry about the accident and that it was more important to make sure he was okay. He waved me off and said that he was good. He didn't leave in anger. What he was doing was protecting something he believed had value for him, his friends and the school. He was not going to allow himself to be the cause of scrutiny for our club or its demise.

"Kevin, tell Manny I've got to let the principal know," I said.

"It won't do any good. He will deny it. He's like that. Loyal, ya know?" Kevin replied.

CHAPTER 5 – Trust the child...

The longest month of the school year was March, dubbed *the long march* or *march of death* by many of my colleagues. It was a time where many teachers, including myself, started to feel the exhaustion and burnout. I spent every waking moment with my students and when I wasn't with them, I was talking about my experiences with them to anyone that would listen; namely my wife. Even she was running out of patience.

"Honey really? Can we talk about something else? Anything else!?"

Maybe my job was consuming me or maybe I was just passionate. Regardless, I knew I had to find a balance soon before personal burn out set in. Maybe I just needed to get out of school. Maybe a field trip was in order.

Field trips were a logistical and financial conundrum; a nightmare to some degree. NYC public transit has its own assortment of challenges when navigated solo. Imagine adding over 50 teenagers to the mix, trying to get them all to the station, down the stairs onto the platform and then into the same train car **and** being mindful of the other passengers.

* * *

Students have as much to teach their teachers as to learn from them. I often felt a responsibility to have all the answers and developed an almost paternal instinct to protect them from criticism, especially by outsiders. A mind focused on a defensive posture loses the flexibility it needs to resolve conflict and facilitate a change in hearts and minds. I forgot this important lesson on our way to midtown. This was when my students surprised and humbled me.

"Can you believe this?" snarled a white woman in her early 50's to her equally manicured 40 something year old companion.

"I know, but everyone is allowed on the train." She replied. "Isn't someone controlling them?"

My blood started to boil. I'm not sure if it was their tone, their glares or the word *controlling* said the same way one would about a dog on a leash that set me off. I was livid. I tried to tell myself to breathe. They didn't know my kids. This was just ignorance. I was shaking internally.

Just take a deep breath.

Suddenly, words were falling out of my mouth at these women.

"Excuse me. Hello, ladies. How are you?" I said with my badly concealed anger. I was met with blank stares.

"I couldn't help but notice that there is a rather loud group of white kids right over there and some of my black and brown kids over here. When you made that comment regarding the noise level, I was wondering who you were addressing exactly. Oh, and a brief comment about the word control. It probably wasn't intended, but..."

I couldn't stop myself. As the words were being uttered I regretted the way I went about this. I didn't know if my boys were even paying attention. Then, right on cue, my angry speech was interrupted.

"Excuse me miss. Hello," Brice said, all 6 foot 5 inch, 360 pounds of African American man-child of him. "I just want to apologize for my friends being so loud. We are just pretty excited to get out of school and do something a little more interesting."

The blank stares softened and a conversation began between Brice and these women about where we were headed. Brice taught us all something that day. I was confronting the issue with anger. I wanted to protect my students because I had filtered the situation as a threat. Brice, on the other hand, had the true intent of making peace in his heart. He got the results I wished I had accomplished. Seeking first to understand and show love takes courage. A 14 year old freshman was able to see the world as good and create good in a way I couldn't understand in real time.

* * *

My high school in spring was flooded by the smell of freshly cut grass and the sound of coaches barking instructions as the sports teams took to the field. Bright green leaves broke through the monotony of the gray and brown tree lined backdrop. It was the same thing in my East Harlem school minus the trees, sponsored sports and the smell of fresh anything. For the last three weeks, a decaying rat had been stuck in our radiator filling the room with its stench. Despite all of us being on the verge of vomiting, we seemed to adjust and forget its existence. The human mind is amazing at refocusing attention from such details as the lack of uncontaminated air or the presence of caterpillars.

I decided to take my team to Long Island for the weekend. A little beach and tackle football on something other than a concrete surface would be a welcome break. We all piled into a jeep I had borrowed from a friend and drove out to the quiet area of eastern Long Island I had grown up in. The boys soaked in the open road, sunny skies and peacefulness like astronauts on their first moon landing.

We arrived at my mother's house. The boys got out one by one and I led them to the backyard. We all stood there and stared upward at the trees. Suddenly, Steven yelped.

"What the hell is that?"

"What?" I asked, startled by the break in serenity.

Silken strings with small travelers hung in the air – caterpillars.

It was incredibly easy for me to take these types of things for granted. Steven had never seen a caterpillar in his life. I didn't want to feel pity for his inability to recognize a common bug. Instead, I wanted to facilitate as many experiences as I could for him and the rest of these boys; even if the experience was as simple as the hanging world of caterpillars. We drove to the beach next. I hadn't seen smiles like that since our triumphant journey home from the tournament. Good salty air and water temperatures that knocked the wind out of everybody as we all took a plunge. We hung out until dark and then made our way back to my mother's house to get the sand out of everything before driving to the city.

The landscape off the Long Island Expressway transformed from sand to green to steel and finally, concrete. The familiar sounds of city life hit us all at once. Ramon muttered that it looked different to him.

"How?" asked Steven.

"I don't know, smaller. It's like the more you see the more you want to see and then you realize that your world isn't the whole world."

* * *

On Monday, Ramon came in with sketches for our team's t-shirts. He proudly held up a brolic looking panther. In Jiu Jitsu, it's not uncommon for an animal to represent an academy. A black t-shirt with a strong muscled fighting panther from Harlem seemed like the absolute perfect choice. Each student chipped in 15 dollars to make Ramon's symbol our official uniform. That same week, we made a commitment to compete in our next tournament. It would be in Hoboken; much closer to the city and more opportunity for family and friends to be present. This time, we were not as lucky with negotiating a better team price. Maybe it was the juju that followed us from Za's meltdown in New England or the unexpected wins over some hometown clubs, but either way there wasn't any money for the entry fees.

Once again, the boys organized a fundraising bake sale. The support and turnout was nothing short of miraculous. We had ten parents working alongside the kids to sell home baked goods for their cause. Altogether, we raised 300 dollars and it paid for all the entry fees we needed. Game plans were constructed for all the guys competing that focused on their strengths. Steven would pull guard and utilize his flexibility. George would clamp down and stop opponent movement from mount positions, looking for an opening for the arm bar. Ramon and Brice would overpower their opponents and get points for takedowns, mount and shoulder chokes via arm and head triangles. Hansel, who hadn't taken part in the last tournament, would use his speed and conditioning. Kevin would shoot for takedowns, sprawl against them and play an effective top game. His sweeps were sound and he could maintain mountain top. I knew Kevin was searching for **Tom Fox**, but we had to be conservative until we got our match. Za was a special case. I had to promise not to leave his mat during this competition, so that he would promise not to deviate from the game plan we came up with. Step by step, we went over it every day before the tournament. It was tight and with it, he could win.

* * *

Iron sharpens iron.

Pressure can crush a spirit or it can elevate a soul to shine as bright as a diamond.

Saturday, May 24th was our tournament date. It was posted in the halls, in classrooms and on kids' notebooks. The whole school was vibrating support for our team and my boys were training up to the challenge. I could hear them shouting out some of the very first mantras I used on them, when they were struggling through their 2 mile run.

Pain is just weakness leaving the body!!!

I had implemented a sandbag routine for conditioning and they were lugging homemade 50-100 pound bags up and down the school stairs like UFC champions.

Pain now, glory later!!!

April came and went, much like the last six months. Now, it was time for the glory. I made my ritual speech, played our D12 anthem and entered the gym. GAME DAY!

There were familiar faces at weigh-ins, notably Tom Fox. Kevin shot me a look as I simultaneously did the same. It was a look of determination and confidence. He nodded. We were there to win.

I never left Za's side, as the rest of the guys competed. Andrew coached Steven to silver, George to a bronze and witnessed Ramon, up on points, just gas out. He said he wasn't even tired; that adrenaline got the best of him and that it wouldn't happen again. I knew I could have better mentally prepared him for this big event. I apologized, but he was already planning on how to get ready for the next competition and cheer on the rest of the team. I learned that Brice could have ground out a victory, but he froze after flipping a kid onto the ground. He legitimately thought he had hurt him and just stood there, while his opponent took his back. That was it. He lost on points. The team was incredibly supportive. Not a bad word was said about Brice's performance. He was capable of mauling anyone trying to do harm to someone he cared about, but he just wasn't built to compete. The lessons of self restraint, respect and camaraderie in Jiu Jitsu are what he held close to his heart. Hansel destroyed everyone in his division – takedowns, mounts, and three submissions. Technical and efficient, he took these victories as learning opportunities. He asked if he could do advanced next time.

"I'm not sure if I'll win it all, but I think I have a shot."

Less than 7 months of training and my team had developed into a group of elite division medal hunters.

Definitely time for the glory.

Za and I made final preparations for his matches. His mantra through the play by play of our plan was *Pick them up and put them down, gently.*

Three victories later, all of them carbon copies of each other, I knew he got it.

"I picked them up!!" he exclaimed to me.

"And put them down," I interjected.

"Gently," he added with a massive smile.

A coach from another team passed us and said, "Hey, excuse me. That was technically amazing. Great job out there kid."

"Thanks," Za replied. His smile could have lit the room.

"How much better was that than last time? How much better does it feel to be acknowledged for something positive?" I asked him.

"Much," he replied.

"Is everybody out to get us?" I asked.

"No, not really. Some people are just nice."

If you fight hard and within the rules, you get your props. The mat is one of the great equalizers in life. You are what you do, literally. Nothing else matters.

* * *

Kevin's last match began as Za received his gold medal. The team rallied around the mat. Kevin submitted his first opponent via guillotine off a textbook sprawl. His second match scored via takedowns and establishing solid mounts.

"Ok, Kevin!!"

He looked over and gave me a thumbs up.

Time for Tom.

Third match and shot after shot, sprawl after sprawl, Tom Fox and Kevin battled back and forth. Neither one backed down. Neither one retreated. It was as heart thumping as a scoreless match could be. Our game plan was being executed flawlessly and we were in a dogfight.

One minute left.

"Keep breathing, Kevin!! We've got one minute." I tried to keep my voice as calm as possible even though I was losing it with anticipation.

30 seconds.

"Kevin, it's right now. Double leg. All or nothing, bro!!"

Kevin shot in. Grabbed around the upper thigh and pushed forward. They were almost out of bounds. Takedown! The referee had nano seconds to decide. If they were in bounds, we would get the points. If not, no points and a restart.

"C'mon ref! Give him the points!!" yelled multiple voices from both our team and spectators.

The referee put up his fingers. Points awarded.

Ten seconds.

The bag indicating the match was over was thrown. Kevin, in his tank top and long shorts, sprinted over and jumped into my arms.

"All I heard was you, coach!"

It was bigger than the match. Through his tears, my usually stoic and serious man-child wept, "We did it. Just a kid from the Bronx. Man, we did it!"

Outside of the birth of my child, I have never had such a proud moment in my life. My personal wins on the mat seemed so small. Here, my boys had proven that it didn't matter where you came from or what clothes you wore. It was hard work, natural talent and the relationship between coach and athlete that made the difference. We had validated the entire concept of Jiu Jitsu as I hoped it would be applied in our East Harlem school. Weakness was only a perception. Strength could be learned, harnessed and utilized productively for personal and community victory. Kevin took the medal stand alone, but we all stood up there with him in spirit. None of us were able to hold back our tears nor did we want to.

* * *

June.

It had been the longest 9 month year of my life. The toll of juggling full time graduate school, my first year of teaching and coaching the team would soon be over. As things wound down, I found myself grading state exams. I had the "luck" of grading Kevin's. I scored him three points lower than the second teacher to grade him. I think I had higher expectations, especially since I knew the potential he had on and off the mat.

On the mat, things were also winding down. Practice was now just twice a week. Chris, the student who had called me out so colorfully and made me question my mission as a teacher, had been asking to match with me since the winter. I knew it was really about having the chance to beat up on a teacher. He was now 18 and about to graduate, so I finally obliged.

"Really?" he asked.

"Yup...tomorrow. 3:30. Mats down. No spectators; just me and you. If I tap, you stop. If you tap, I stop. Cool?"

"I'm in!" he replied.

The next day, with a crowd of 40 kids pounding on the locked door to be let in, Chris and I met in my classroom for our bout. I reminded him of the rules. A tap meant it was over. He nodded calmly and maybe with a touch of arrogance.

"Let's do this."

Chris took a swing, a right hand haymaker, and missed. I stepped in for the standing triangle. Brought him down to the mat.

Tap, tap, tap.

"We can go again, if you want," I said to him.

Chris tried again and again and again. Each time we ended up on the mat, he tapped.

Finally, we both stood. I asked him if he was okay.

"Man, you can fight!?" Chris said out of breathe.

"For a white guy?" I joked with a smile.

"For any guy," he answered.

We double slapped bro-hugged to seal the deal. We had reached an understanding. This battle wasn't about humiliation. To borrow the Dog brother's slogan, *Higher enlightenment through harder contact* proved true in East Harlem that afternoon.

* * *

Steven was going to be graduating. He didn't have a lot of options open to him, so I arranged for him to stay with my brother in North Carolina, who would be teaching him a trade. My brother owned several small businesses and a big place in the N. Carolina inlets. I had spoken to him about Steven as well as all the boys and my experiences in East Harlem. I think I may have inspired him, but he wanted to do something to give back. This was his opportunity.

I had spoken with Steven's parents who agreed to the plan even though their child would be hundreds of miles away. Steven was going to develop the technical skills of air conditioning and heating. There were emails and phone calls exchanged between him and my brother. I stayed on the sidelines. I didn't want Steven to feel pressured. This decision to leave the only place he had ever known was difficult enough without having his mentor interfering.

The last week of school, he came to my classroom with an odd look on his face.

"Hey Mr. B, can we talk?"

"What's up?" I asked.

"I'm a little nervous. I've never been to North Carolina, never lived outside of the city. You really think I can do this?"

"Steven, think about this year. Think about everything you've had to overcome to get your medals; to graduate. You have a strength I wish I knew I had when I was your age and even now. You went through a war and made it out on the other side stronger than when you started. I have no doubt you can succeed at anything you put your mind to. I wouldn't have set this up with my brother if I didn't believe that."

I couldn't make this decision for him. I couldn't make him see what I saw.

"The question is, do **you** believe it?" I finally asked him.

Steven looked at me with a fixed gaze; his eyes deep in thought. Perhaps he was replaying the events of the last 9 months that brought him to this point. Perhaps he was thinking about those caterpillars and all the new experiences that he could have if he decided to venture into the unknown. After a very long pause, his gaze cleared and he was fully present.

"You know what, I do. Thanks."

With that, he walked off.

EPILOGUE

A few words from members of the East Harlem Jiu Jitsu club, now in their mid to late twenties.

Kevin

Do you remember the first time we met? Miguel asked me to come see this "jujitsu class". In my head I thought, yea 2 dudes grabbing each other I'm good. So since I had nothing better to do I went to watch. As I was standing there watching my friend get his butt whipped I gave you a face like you can't be that tough. And it was as if you read my face and you said wanna roll. I laughed and said nah I'm good. You kept on so I said alright. After getting my butt whipped and my shirt stretched out I said to myself I will 1 day be good enough to beat this guy. I will beat him with the first move he used on me and that was with the rear naked choke. Even though I never got good enough to beat you I became good enough to be the captain of your jujitsu team. If anyone ever grappled with me then they know that the same move pj first used on me became my signature move and I most likely made them tap to it. My daughter Miley is now old enough that she has asked me to teach her a few moves. I always laugh and say babe daddy doesn't do that stuff anymore. She replies well show me what you remember and I always teach her the basics. The shrimp and roll, if someone is on top of you hips to the sky, someone shoots for you sprawl back to control them. When in control I have taught her the 3 basic arm bars, a leg lock and of course the rear naked choke. What's crazy is that what I learned over 11 years ago as a sport can some day save my daughter's life. The basic things that I teach her now will always be imprinted in her forever. So thanks P.J cause what you taught me has successfully been handed down to the next generation of Rivera's. Oh yea and we always look through that grappling book I won in that in house jujitsu tournament.

Ramon

PJ can make anything interesting and seems interested in everything. Any student would be lucky to be instructed by a teacher who can educate without putting the class to sleep. PJ is a person who actually cares about the young people he works with.

(*top left to bottom right:* Andrew, Kevin, Miguel, Steven, Za and George)

About the Authors

PaulJames A. Bekanich
Instagram: @bodhisrc
BLOG: https://zenvalhallajiujitsu.wordpress.com/

PJ started grappling in 1994. He has trained with many of the greatest instructors in the world including Pedro Sauer, Renzo Gracie, Sambo Steve, Murillo Santana, Jorge Gurgel, Cassio Werneck, Luis Melo and Junior Elado.

He holds Masters Degrees from Fordham University and George Washington University. He has used education and his experience since 2003 to work with kids and to build community as a teacher and school administrator. He currently works with the Secret Roll Club (SRC) planning open mat events and developing a youth program to spread the word of Jiu Jitsu. When not working on improving the public education system and training, he spends time loving and laughing with his daughter, meditating to find the balance of Nirvana and Valhalla and thinking about new ways Jiu Jitsu can make the world a better place.

Julia Fragias
Instagram: @tojulaki
BLOG - https://juliafragiaslmt.wordpress.com/

Julia holds a BA in English Writing, an Occupational Studies Degree in Massage Therapy and multiple certificates in corrective fitness and mobility. She has been writing about all subjects related to health and wellness since 2012. She is a passionate supporter of the Jiu Jitsu community and has trained in the martial art of Muay Thai. She collaborated with her friend PJ on this book to help tell the story of how Jiu Jitsu saved the lives of these at risk teens and to a large extent, that of their teacher and coach.

Julia currently lives in south Brooklyn and is pursuing graduate studies in Psychology.

Made in the USA
Coppell, TX
07 November 2024

39795288R00030